A NEW SILENCE

Joseph Massey

ALSO BY JOSEPH MASSEY

Full-length books:
Illocality (Wave Books, 2015)
To Keep Time (Omnidawn, 2014)
At the Point (Shearsman Books, 2011)
Areas of Fog (Shearsman Books, 2009)

Chapbooks:
Minima St. (Range, 2003)
Eureka Slough (Effing Press, 2005)
Bramble (Hot Whiskey, 2005)
Property Line (Fewer & Further, 2006)
November Graph (Longhouse, 2007)
Out of Light (Kitchen Press, 2008)
Within Hours (Fault Line Press, 2008)
The Lack Of (Nasturtium Press, 2009)
Exit North (Book Thug, 2010)
Mock Orange (Longhouse, 2010)
Another Rehearsal for Morning (Longhouse, 2011)
Thaw Compass (Press Board Press, 2014)
An Interim (Tungsten Press, 2014)
What Follows (Ornithopter Press, 2015)
Present Conditions (Hollyridge Press, 2018)
Five Poems (Tungsten Press, 2018)

A NEW SILENCE

SHEARSMAN BOOKS

First published in the United Kingdom in 2019 by
Shearsman Books
50 Westons Hill Drive
Emersons Green
BRISTOL
BS16 7DF

Shearsman Books Ltd Registered Office
30–31 St. James Place, Mangotsfield, Bristol BS16 9JB
(this address not for correspondence)

www.shearsman.com

ISBN 978-1-84861-671-4

Cover: "None Too Soon," Wendy Heldmann
Book Design: LK James

"We all have moments with the dust, but the dew is given."

—EMILY DICKINSON

Contents

For the Margin -------------------------------- *3*

*

The Reprieve -------------------------------- *7*
Present Conditions -------------------------- *9*
Reaches -------------------------------------- *10*
Circumference -------------------------------- *12*
Late March ---------------------------------- *14*
Sudden Bridge -------------------------------- *16*
Vigil -- *18*
Forced Perspective -------------------------- *19*
Otherwise ------------------------------------ *20*
Blinds --------------------------------------- *22*
Brookside ------------------------------------ *30*
Plein Air ------------------------------------ *31*

*

On the Solstice ------------------------------ *35*
An Offering ---------------------------------- *37*
Nothing More -------------------------------- *38*
Heat Index ----------------------------------- *40*
Clear -- *48*
The Work ------------------------------------- *49*
The Practice --------------------------------- *50*
For a Failed Suicide ------------------------- *52*
Fifth Floor ---------------------------------- *54*
Called Back ---------------------------------- *55*
One Month Later ----------------------------- *56*
Early Dark ----------------------------------- *57*
What Follows --------------------------------- *67*

*

A Line Through October ------------------71
Distortion and Late October---------------82
Pleasant St. -------------------------------83
Garden Level-------------------------------84
Holy Name --------------------------------91
House at Night-----------------------------92
Placeholder --------------------------------94
In Closing ----------------------------------95
Outside In ---------------------------------96

*

A Window in New England ------------- 101

*

Without--------------------------------------- 127
Main St. -------------------------------------- 128
Between Seasons----------------------------- 129
Early Fall ------------------------------------- 131
Northern Tracks----------------------------- 133
After Trakl------------------------------------ 137
Nashawannuck ------------------------------ 138
Amulet (Midwinter)------------------------- 139
March, Closer -------------------------------- 143
These Days------------------------------------ 144
Old Song-------------------------------------- 145
Notes on a Dead End------------------------ 146

*

To the Reader------------------------------- 151

For the Margin

Night leaves in its wake
a voice I don't recognize;
an echo flagging
in cold, bent
by cold

and the dull thud
of a 40 watt bulb.

At the seam
of panic
dawn erodes
the hour

while I wait for you,
the nameless,
to pronounce
the hollow

of what I'm not—

the poem
you already are.

The Reprieve

A week
that freezes, thaws,
and freezes again.

The skyline scales
and cracks.
Morning's frayed

gray plumes
pull through the wreck
and the wreck in mind.

To be reminded
there's grace
in ordinary weather,

in the reprieve
from neon
and clouds low enough

to cloud thought. Grace
in daylight, the drowse
and sway;

and how, when it's this
thin, things barely cling
to their names. Grace

to be nameless, a form
among forms, drifting
in January glare.

Grace, too,
when windows
reflect and distort,

at night,
the shape of a room.

Present Conditions

Today the weather within
is the weather without.
Even the wind is broken,
stammering over gnarled stalks
and black bulbs punctured through
snowpack. I'm alive
in the contrast, dragging myself
from a dream, eyes adjusting
to the bright. In a semaphore
of stripped limbs
the sun, segmented, multiplies.

Reaches

The draft that lifts the page

slips through
solid wall, evades

an origin.

•

It isn't like anything else—
this monochrome expanse

at the edge of March. Cloud
frozen above a public works lot.

How far now below zero.

•

Monday's bottom-upped sun

scumbles over new snow

and your face, leaving
only eyes at the center.

•

All the ghosts out
in the open.

Circumference

Notice the damage
arranged in rhythms
that mimic
cohesion, edges
we think
to find our grip.
The way rain
decodes snow
banked against
the curb
—sewer grate
caked with mud:
a few small nouns
stuck there. Notice
traffic's under-
current of
static, silence
(as close as we
come to it) parcels
into speech. Notice
the sunbeam
split four ways
by a spent shrub

at the end of
an alley—all
of its rubble
sagging into
gravel, pinned
to the flash.

Late March

And the mud again
ripped open

at the seams, silver
in afternoon's glow-

ering shine. Sunday
slowly implodes

into itself: the hollow
of a vowel humming

under the surface
we strain to pull

our voice—
a voice—through.

We've endured
a certain dormancy

and arrived in time
(out of time) to say it.

To imagine we've
said it, that it

could be enough.

Sudden Bridge

At the slack edge
of spring, the day

falls behind and
ahead of itself.

Stunted sumac under-
lines abandoned

factory stacks;
bricks flaking

into sky. Turn,
see blue graffiti

ghost concrete—
cracked slab banking

a seasonal creek.
Beneath dammed-up limbs

a toppled yield sign
flickers, and your face

flickers, crossing
the street, in glare

from a guardrail.

Vigil

A contrail arcs
over the wreck. Snowbanks
returned to gravel; litter
and its language
ground to grit. This excuse
for spring. Nothing to see
beyond a blind spot
collapsing into afterimage.
Nothing to hear beyond a voice
consuming itself in an alley.
How the world expands
as a thought expands
with the angle of the season.
Between parking block
and dumpster
crocuses clarify
their square of shade.

Forced Perspective

Alley
outlined
in purple
loosestrife.

Bewilderment—

imagine it
possessed
a tint.

Otherwise

Posthumous in spring, I

collapse into other
rhythms, colors

—a palette unspooled

at the speed of
dreaming. Forsythia

web each edge
and edgeless gap

of a condemned home.
A row of them

strained into a season
where I stand

ahead of where
I stood, the shell

of a word,

of the air,

of what was
or wasn't said.

Blinds

To listen
is to see

when the light
is a thing

felt in the ear—
it rings

you awake.

A dream's jagged
remains, what
morning absorbs.

Light, only light,
in place of nothing
left to remember.

Cliff face
shaded in
April snow
that fell
for an hour
overnight.

Off the highway
a stand of birch slants

above a vernal pool.
Sight slows to hold

flaked white
raked through

a stretched wreck of landscape.

A tree as thin
as your wrist

sprays
from the split

in a river rock.

A flag's reflection
dents the
water,

blurs
the debris,
mostly leaves.

When shadow
ingests shadow

and road clatter
thins into crickets.

When the notebook's
margins are lost

and language
sprawls. When

windows turn
brown, vacant

in their glare.

I return
to my body

attached to
a long vowel

stretched
between us.

Brookside

The air, the dull glow of humidity; gnats and flies fray the corners, flash peripherally. Peeper chants pump from the other side of the brook, their dark pocket. When we stop talking, nothing else does. When language leaves us, how many other languages drum from the margins to reorganize the silence.

•

The world is what exceeds the capacity of our senses—the unseen momentum—this bright spillage ringing the day.

•

Pollen-skinned pond's edge by the dock where we stood and tried to describe it—as yellow as the memory of yellow, a memory of light without context. We gave up and just looked. And walked further.

Plein Air

Forsythia
flood my vision—

the yellow world
flashing caution.

On the Solstice

Heat lightning
stilts the gloam

and lingers
in the inner-eye.

This negotiation
between stasis
and abrasion,

petrichor
and car exhaust.

I move through
the room

or the room
moves through me

while night draws back
into insect static.

Air too thick to think

and the moon in a pool
on stained linoleum.

An Offering

Candle flame flinches
against the breath
I forgot I was breathing,
caught in August's exhale.
To see a thing clearly, listen
to the silence it inhabits.
Listen as traffic translates rain
into an open syllable
stretched toward the horizon.
Sit still in a still room
and watch weather pixelate
a window. Watch orange roses
in a makeshift vase
wilt on the sill.
This, too,
is a form of devotion.

Nothing More

Clover mite crushed
    under my finger, red
streak dragged over a blank
    page, as blank
as the hour, the day,
    despite the low hum
in the apartment:
    refrigerator motor
kicking on, the old man
    across the hall talking
to himself. It isn't enough
    to write into this
vacancy, to say
    the day's blank—
but what else is summer:
    what doesn't heat hollow
and reduce to a streak—
    these blown husks
striking pavement,
    a wasp trapped
between panes of glass.
    Leave the page stained.
A book of stains.

The room dissolving
around a bolt of sun
    slashed down the wall.

Heat Index

An hour
before sunset

crickets loop

both sides
of the street

—a rattle
of constant recoil.

When memory sifts
the season, a tone
too thin to measure

remains. Outside
it's too hot for memory,

too humid for thought.

Even these half-dead
dandelions, scattered

around the entrance
of an abandoned Bank
of America, startle

into the present.

This far into August
what doesn't come undone?

Thunder brackets the lull.

A ribbon of gnats
rotates around a street lamp.

The only relief is sleep.

And in the morning shadows
evaporate
before touching ground.

The mountain
a shard of gravel
propped against the horizon.

A bird or a cloud could dislodge it.

I'm tired
of living
window
to window,

keeping time
by how dim
or how bright.

Sepia beams
cross and
recross the floor.

The darkness lengthens.

Night offered
a moth

banging around
a lamp.

When the mind
consents to mirror

the pond's surface
suddenly still.

A reprieve
from fragments,

summer's
insistence,

what punctures
stammering

sun, gauzy
wind. Let

vision catch
a wasp

braiding space
between wrought

iron handrails
in front of

the senior center.
Let vision

rove without
a thought

to anchor it.
All senses see.

Now I've walked
far enough

to locate
where dusk

begins, the
block where

my world ends.
Peeper trill

and electric
insect whir

pump from
overgrown grass

a liquor store's
red neon

signage stains.

Clear

After eight days of rain
what isn't overwritten
under sun. These

asphalt cracks
pushed further apart.
Eight days without

definition: gray walled
the room in, and I
thought I found a way

to stop thinking—to allow
gray to become a sound
I couldn't hum myself out of.

All I heard was a window.
A long weed beat
unevenly against it.

The Work

Summer is a ritual of endurance. The way rain rewinds into
haze no color cuts through. Even the tiger lilies surrounding
the supermarket parking lot are washed out, mute. Today's
forecast: suffocation. You have to strain to catch the signal that
ignites the voice flowering beyond the brain—a language you
hardly know as your own, but it is yours. You stand outside
the poem, tend to its edges. Worry the seams. Keep it from
collapsing. This is the work you've been given. A power line in
the fog, sloping toward infinity.

The Practice

Panic, the speechless
hour, blooms
in dust—

a spent web
vibrating
in a corner.

Where am I
without a word
to hold against
the day,

to witness
transparency
as prayer
and ballast.

Afternoon dark
as late dusk.
I listen
to thunder

hollow
the particular
silence of hail

raining
against glass.

My mind
finally removed
from the room

dissolves
in outside sound.

For a Failed Suicide

How many days
since I last left my body.

Spring happened
but I didn't notice,

caught in an echo
that refused
to unremember.

I thought
I'd die to stop thinking.

I woke
in a locked ward.

My mind grazed
on a grid:

windows enforced
with wire mesh.
I knew I wasn't dead

when the colors came back.

Green hills
underscored
by cold linoleum.

Fifth Floor

No one's walking
the hall. The ghost of a code
clings to a chalkboard
on a beige wall. Fluorescent
light vibrates my eyes.

This is what counts for silence.
The building's gills
breathing out.

Even the old man mumbling
the same fractured phrase
without pause
into a paper cup
becomes a kind of white noise.

Behind him
tinted windows
turn a world to winter.

Called Back

I'm still a body
after a season spent

dying to leave it.
Was it winter

or spring, or the weeks
when they blend—

a sub-season
of mud, puddles

that froze overnight
and the next day,

half-melted, spiked
the sky's reflection.

One Month Later

My mouth still moves
around a language

that baffles me alive.
My vision's blurred

but wherever I look
a world wakes.

I sit for hours
chanting in silence

the name of each thing
attached to each shadow

waving slowly
over white stucco.

Early Dark

A vein along the road poised to spill.

Red leaves rim
a creek running
under a footbridge.

I haven't moved this afternoon

reading a guardrail
scarred with hieroglyphs.

Things and the names of things
sinking into sepia,

       cold shadow
stitched to cracked asphalt.

Silence isn't
a question—
isn't an answer—

isn't even itself.

Overgrown grass
in the margin
of an alley

palpitates
without wind.

Water bending
into light, light
bending into time.

Edges engorged
by an orange undertone.

Within one thought or another,
one weather or another, we're always
almost here.

In the time it takes to look:
the surface of the pond
blurs a world back together.

To know the season

the depth of its cut
by touch—
a tone

unfolding
an echo.

Elision, the early dark

after summer's
serrated glare

made seeing
sting.

Snow slants through
peaked leaves,
power lines—

that gap where
nothing's said.

A vein along the road poised to spill.

What Follows

To arrive at a kind of quiet
that won't recoil into speech

or uncoil into music, illegible
as dusk and its marginalia.

Mind is place
and world, pieces—

how one runs into another, another.
Remember the dark as it creases the dark

could be any animal.

A Line Through October

September gone
in gray rain slash,
gutters sift
fallen color, but how

to pronounce
October
when streets seethe
sepia, echo summer

what binds the day
to belief, what binds
belief to perception,
at the seam

between seasons
when words blur, phrases
warp, the sentence
surrounding us dissolves

slant October light
supplants the itch
to think anything
beyond light

and what light
laves
to name
and measure

at the threshold
of the present
this shadow
is the mind's shadow

shielding a noun
in the mulch, half-
buried, decayed
beyond a name

dawn signals
the language
a world wakes within—
a capillary bloom

of wet, red leaves
imprinting haze
too thin
to be fog

the room
sheds the room
as dusk sweeps
through, a leaf-

spiked shadow
stretched from
floor
to ceiling

candles voice
evening, these
shadows phrased
across the wall,

this exile,
in the cell where
I breathe
myself blank

the synesthesia
of the season,
an off-kilter walk
through *the Shower*

of Stain, vision
enveloped
as sound
a slow shattering inward

late bees needle
late flowers
hovering over a sidewalk
cracked into hieroglyphs

these ribboned
bee shadows
decipher
as a kind of silence

other echoes inhabit
the alley, summer's alley,
enclosed now by October's
gloaming, the bled sky

gaping above
lopsided sheds
sheathed in yellow
hollowing orange

from a caved-in
photocopy shop
sparrows cast a crooked line
on their way to invoke

other omens—
a month of omens
looming
in each color-ticked margin

Distortion and Late October

Leafless maples—
I know their shape—
blur through glass
and crosshatch
my chest. Sick
of looking, I
close the blinds
and wait
for the pills
to take effect.
This isn't the room
I remember,
but the walls fall
in their familiar way.
Night enough now
for the window
to reflect
my face
caved in
with lamplight.

Pleasant St.

      Flood lights glaze the facade
of a funeral home—no

               moon, no neon, only this
to mark and manifest night.

Garden Level

Night gives nothing back; it only appears to cohere. What's locked in dissolves without pause. An animal rattles mulch and twice-dead leaves piled against the window. I know the walls are there for the sounds they sift into the room—the room that inhabits me—underground.

Sun in the shape of a quadrangle on a wood floor. Curtains blown horizontal split it in half. Dust divots air, dents the pale afternoon. An hour isn't like anything, not even itself. A window, a patch of lawn, a street for the tide of its noise, for measure. A stream of particulars undoing the room.

It can take all day to filter out the debris of a dream, to see a thing contained by its terms. Call it clarity. You have to almost stop thinking; get up to the edge of the clanging at the back of the brain. Go dumb to the light.

Three weeks in and the season begins to click. Weather to word; word to weather. A bird circles, punctuates a bloodless sky— the husk we're under. The street a monochrome stream. Cold enough to numb thought.

Snow light at dusk, the deepening bruise; a blue that hums. A soundless ringing between the eyes where all things sink and disperse. For once we're reading the world without the names by which we dream it. Nothing to say; nothing saying us.

Everything comes to a point along the horizon; every limb stripped to a line. Even the clouds sharpen, shaved against a mountain. A pond duplicates the scene—if your gaze drops. To suspend the senses in the drone of geometry. To forget the traffic here.

The way the mind bends to receive injured weather, the sudden warmth, as though half awake and watching a place—a room, a field—assemble itself one object at a time. A syntax expanding beneath fanned rays of gaping sun. Center everywhere, circumference nowhere.

Holy Name

Funeral bagpipes blare
a cleft through the cold.

Notes absorbed in monochrome—

maples (what red
remains) agitate
the edge.

House at Night

Stranded
by speech, nouns
twine to amplify

the asphalt-kindled
dark.

*

Who isn't
inhabits the house—

the husk
of what wasn't

where a lamp-lit window
hangs.

*

Sidewalk crabgrass
collars a fire hydrant

collared by street light.

Gnarled cactus
in a pot on a sill.

*

Silence is revision

of silence, the sound
of a paper cup

dumping shadow
over a curb.

Placeholder

Now that the animal
trapped in the rafters

is silent, the cold alone

is a sound.
February's glare

bent by Victorian glass

casts the outline
of a spike of ice

spread from floor to ceiling—

the only thing
holding the house up.

In Closing

Frozen rain
    rattles the window
        over the bed. No

silence left
    to swallow—
        the room fills

with what
    it can't contain.
        A mouth open

at the brink of
    the breath of
        a phrase

only the wall
    knows how
        to pronounce.

The wall
    pinned tight
        to a shadow.

Outside In

A path of overlapping
roots, shallow
gravel pile—

an orange
rind hung up
in webbed brush.

Voice doesn't fail
to fall to vision
while sundown's

serrated gauze
draws the breath
against itself. Barely

enough sun now
to cinch together
this run-on sentence

of objects reaching
to be seen
to organize the field.

A few leaves
twist and spit back

at light, thin
as it is, light.

A Window in New England

Noun by noun dusk draws
down night, a singular thing-
lessness, an open
syllable pronouncing lack.
How breath alone becomes sight.

Call it November—
the mountain carved flat by fog;
the bottomed-out clouds
refusing metaphor, no
language left to contain them.

This morning the light
is bleached by cold. Pinhole sun
caught up in clear quartz.
Blinded, I read the quiet
unwriting frost, field, fence, gull.

Church bells bend into
syllables, into patterns:
these leafless shadows
on the lawn clawing toward
asphalt, dispersing the day.

Now the room contains
the season, its signs inscribe
the wall, ink their way
across. When wind litters air
the lines vibrate—the room moves.

A silence beyond
mind, beyond thought. The way air
and light hum soundless-
ly over a field patched with
frost. The way vision listens.

Call it December—
skyline abbreviated
by a rogue cloud deck.
Dead leaves rattle through traffic.
Another world closes in.

Nothing to pronounce
but morning's disorder. What
the dark sifts into
light: the room and its corners—
this illegible shadow.

On the cusp of June
the sun's already August.
Peripheral bees
at the speed of memory
indent the humidity.

Half the mountain drenched
in cloud shadow, the other
green as a thought of
green, an afterthought of green,
the green that remains of green.

Rain that wasn't fore-
casted streaks the afternoon
blind, a blurred version
of a world we imagine
we haven't imagined there.

Distracted by hail
strafing the window, I lost
the silence centered
between my eyes. But silence—
listen—has nowhere to go.

There is no poem
if the breath doesn't tether
to a phrase, suspend-
ing the day in its silence,
collapsing time to a word.

As if Niedecker
were a verb: her chiseled breath,
how it palpitates
the page. To find company
in silence turning a phrase.

How morning coheres
even as a dream repeats
behind my open
eyes: paper blinds leak light, un-
write the dark that gripped the room.

Cid said poverty's
a gift, the ground and the grist
for poetry. Cid
was wrong. How does anyone
catch enough breath from nothing?

After how many
days spent in fluorescent light,
a spray of lilacs
scars my vision while I walk
around the chapel garden.

Almost August, heat
hangs breath-heavy wherever
we walk, even shade
suffocates thought, and language—
this nonsense syllable—wilts.

It isn't these name-
less flowers unfolding from
a narrow alley,
it's the weeds, long and knotted,
that give their rhythm to shade.

Pond's edge pocked white with
cottonwood fluff. Wind-scattered
litter drifts: a spent
condom lost now in pollen—
sluggish current curving green.

There's no metaphor
here. The sky in the pothole
is the sky I see—
I write to say I've seen it.
Long clouds suspended in oil.

Out of the air of
the page—to draw enough breath—
to speak quietly
so that you might mishear me—
and hold the poem open.

Allow the poem
to do your breathing for you—
and forget the breath
in the wake of a language
you know now to be your own.

Without

Sunday is dust
revolving
through slit curtains.

A blank page
bright as an ambulance
churning the humidity.

I've waited hours now

for the room to recede,
for dusk.

For the windows
to go blind.

Main St.

A passing siren
abbreviates panic,
removes me from thinking's
constant throb. Yellowjackets
carve a circular blur
around a soda can
standing in
pissed-on woodchips.
Nostalgia wanes
when it's this hot, when speech
contracts to half a breath
behind a word that won't come.
So humid
even the concrete wilts.

Between Seasons

Morning dilates
a window
flanked by an unkempt hedge.

June arrived and the glare
grew particulate—thick

with gnats
collapsing
around the frame.

I've been indoors
for weeks, but old glass

warps the seam. Shade
spills over asphalt;

clover packs a long fracture.

I'm grounded in these images

that slip
past the screen.

A room where a voice
throws itself in silence

and silence returns
at the edge of a word.

Early Fall

Rain decays dawn—
everything in the yard

leaning, beaded, broken in.
A lucid dream

      the weather
assembles; a pain particular

as light seeping
into an alley

narrowed by overgrowth.
To articulate what slips

the instant
speech moves

to apprehend it.

Cinder blocks stacked
by a metal shed door

totem-like
in haze
of evaporated rain.

Northern Tracks

Ferns flash dark,
chafe train windows
relieved by graffiti:
faded white runes
scrawled on
an underpass slant.
Barbed-wire fence
wrapped around
cracked concrete,
crabgrass, green
plastic bags
ballooning light.
A sign reads
SPECIAL METALS
as we coast into
a ghost town—
half a ghost,
at least, lingering.
Every window
in every building
broken—one
with a branch
lanced into it.

Tree and house
fused, as if
attached
to the same
decaying root
system. A freight
train passes
in the opposite
direction, loaded
with fertilizer:
green and white
sacks stacked and
blurred into blue
that looks
like memory,
a memory
barely there,
washed out—
still enough
to sting. How
sight stings when
things scroll
at this speed;
particulars
particlized.
Yellow sweep
of brown,

of black,
of summer
that hasn't
released into
fall. First
day of fall,
today—
muggy and
bright. But
the air's
hollow edge
foreshadows
October. Now
the car's
flanked by
factories
in pieces
weeds and
abandoned
mattresses
cinch together.
It's true: No-
thing's un-
inhabited. No-
thing goes un-
reclaimed. Red
leaves radiate

in dense brush
bordering woods.
Red sticks
to my peripheral
vision, stains it,
while highway
streaks horizon:
red striations
thread the glare.
Slow, close
to a station.
Algae skirts
a brick wall's
bent reflection
where pond
meets mud,
knotted brush,
roots buckled
aboveground.
The view opens—
opening completely
to the Connecticut
River; the surface
wrinkling what's
left of the day.

After Trakl

When weather gives permission to forget

When the outline of the field reels like a flame and folds in

When the mountains rust into a past-tense sky;

       horizon dim as memory

When October gloam corrals in an alley and I sift it for a phrase

       to contain night, to cloak the mind quiet

When voices overwhelm the dark overwhelming the room

When all I'll know of summer, soon, is a tone gone hollow

       —a sun too small to see

Nashawannuck

All ice, the pond is rough
with half-sunk sticks,
branches, a past season's detritus.

The mangled calligraphy
made legible
by a gathering silence. Now snow

sweeps out across the pond
aligned with a field
aligned with a cemetery, seamless—

seamless
as though a world
were there to be unwritten.

Amulet (Midwinter)

All day rain returns snow
to lawn and asphalt.

Potholes mirror
the low sky's
dead eye—

gray glare
without variation
in a variable wind.

Iced-over branches graph
the oncoming gloom;

the deepening blue

I mistook for dawn
drawn between overlapping lines.

A ritual silence dissolves night
into day, ballasts me
to the room

bludgeoned
by winter's nothing.

Traffic's shadow wobbles
on the far wall. In the window

a garland of late gulls struggle
to cleave a shape from the cold.

March, Closer

Around the edges the gleam
deepens, you'll see it—
the sting of it—

if you look long enough.
A new season bends

and bleeds through
what was wild.
The field

illegible
with language.

We're surrounded

by an exhaustion
of green
gouged out

by gray,
and a pothole
full of melted ice

reassembling sky.

These Days

Hungover, I watch wind compose a world too bright to comprehend: sidewalk scabbed with rock salt, thick shadow thrashed thin through traffic. From this angle the road's a knot gone slack. I wait to cross while gulls shuffle north over a closed Chinese restaurant—the worn white sign and worn white wings, an unfinished phrase dissolving in air.

•

I spent the afternoon sifting through a dream—bright rubble of syllables—for a voice to counter the rain.

•

These days are faceless. The hours monochrome. I talk to myself, as I'm talking now, to drown the sound of thought, to claim a space where nothing hums—where I go breathless, and you are all that's left.

Old Song

The patterns
we're patterned by

disorganize
in silence.

Listen

while late
March light

replaces
the page

with pitch-black
shadow.

Notes on a Dead End

Words won't cohere
around an echo's
leftover pulse:
a car alarm
gone quiet

in an otherwise barren
parking lot at dusk—

barren but for an aura
levitating a dumpster;

asphalt softened
into orange; dead
leaves crushed,
dim confetti.

Gravel, mud,
filthy slush—
there isn't a phrase
to be found here.

A tangle of names

gaze blank
through blank cold.

To the Reader

The breath that breathed into this vacancy
is the same breath breathing you now.
The breath that animates the language

      silence returns to air—

I know no other you to speak to.
I see by the sounds I make in the dark
to reach you—

      to share in the failure

the poem becomes. A conversation
circumambulates an absence
that is its own call
and response, and binds us here
to the page, the room,
for as long as an echo lasts.

ACKNOWLEDGMENTS

A New Silence was written with the grace and blessings of my teacher, Avatar Adi Da Samraj.

Love and thanks to the friends who helped me keep my head above water so I could find the breath to write these poems.

Some versions of these poems first appeared in *Bennington Review, The Cossack Review, Cloud Rodeo, Diagram, Eborakon, EcoTheo Review, Fou, GeoHumanities, Hyperallergic, Jubilat, Matter, Morning Star, Poem-a-Day, Poetry Daily, Spoon River Poetry Review, Supplement, Talisman, Thoreau Society Bulletin,* and *Wave Composition.*

"Present Conditions," "Late March," and "Nashawannuck," first appeared from Tungsten Press as letterpress broadsides.

"Reaches" first appeared as a letterpress broadside from Robinson Press at the Kelly Writers House.

A handful of these poems were published as a chapbook titled *What Follows* by Ornithopter Press.

Another handful of these poems were published as a chapbook titled *Present Conditions* by Hollyridge Press.

And yet another handful of these poems were published as a chapbook titled *Five Poems* by Tungsten Press.

"Center everywhere, circumference nowhere" was plucked with respect from Paramhansa Yogananda's *Autobiography of a Yogi*.

CPSIA information can be obtained
at www.ICGtesting.com
Printed in the USA
LVHW101731180122
708789LV00011B/441